More! Instant Bible Lessons for Preschoolers

Being My Best for God

Pamela J. Kuhn

Rainbow Publishers

Rainbow Publishers • P.O. Box 261129 • San Diego, CA 92196
www.rainbowpublishers.com

To my sweet Landon Reese Clemens:
What a joy you brought this grandma in March of 2006 when you arrived! Your sparkling blue eyes talk to me, and they make think of the kind and gentle love of Jesus. You are my sunshine.
Love, Grandma

MORE! INSTANT BIBLE LESSONS FOR PRESCHOOLERS: BEING MY BEST FOR GOD
©2010 by Rainbow Publishers, first printing
ISBN 10: 1-58411-071-6
ISBN 13: 978-1-58411-071-2
Rainbow reorder# RB36857
RELIGION / Christian Ministry / Children

Rainbow Publishers
P.O. Box 261129
San Diego, CA 92196
www.rainbowpublishers.com

Interior Illustrator: Hallie Gillett
Cover Illustrator: Tammie Lyon

Scriptures are from the *Holy Bible: New International Version* (North American Edition), ©1973, 1978, 1984 by the International Bible Society. Used by permission of Zondervan Bible Publishers.

Printed in the United States of America

Contents

Introduction

Wecome to *Being My Best for God*, a book packed full with useful lesson activities for your preschoolers. You'll find the lively Bible stories and kid-friendly activities make it easy to teach valuable character traits like kindness and honesty. Engage your students with active games and songs, set to familiar melodies, along with age-appropriate puzzles and worksheets. You'll find clear directions and lists of materials for the crafts and snacks, so you'll always be ready to go.

Each of the first eight chapters includes a Bible story, memory verse and numerous activities to help reinforce the lessons about being your best for God. An additional chapter contains projects that can be used anytime throughout the study or at the end to review the lessons. Teacher aids, including bulletin board ideas and discussion starters, are also sprinkled throughout the book.

The most exciting aspect of the *More! Instant Bible Lessons for Preschoolers* series is its flexibility. You can easily adapt these lessons to a Sunday School hour, a children's church service, a Wednesday night Bible study, a Christian school classroom or family home use. And, because there is a variety of reproducible ideas from which to choose, you will enjoy creating a class session that is best for your group — whether large or small, beginning or advanced, active or studious.

This book is written to add fun and uniqueness to learning about being your best for God. Teaching children is exciting and rewarding, especially when you successfully share God's Word and its principles with your students. *More! Instant Bible Lessons for Preschoolers* will help you accomplish that goal. Blessings on you as your students learn how to be their best for God.

How to Use This Book

Each chapter begins with a Bible story for you to read to your class, followed by discussion questions. Then, use any or all of the activities in the chapter to help drive home the message of that lesson. Each activity is tagged with one of the icons below, so you can quickly flip through the chapter and select the projects you need. Simply cut off the teacher instructions on the pages and duplicate as desired.

craft   finger play   teacher help   bulletin board   activity

puzzle   action song   song   game   snack

Chapter 1
God Wants Me to Be Happy, Not Jealous

 ## Memory Verse

In your anger do not sin. Ephesians 4:26

Story to Share
God Likes You Best

After God sent Adam and Eve out of the Garden of Eden because they had sinned, they set up a new home. They had a son named Cain, then they had another son named Abel.

Adam and Eve taught the boys to work. Abel became a shepherd and took care of the sheep. Cain liked to farm the fields, growing grain and fruit.

Adam and Eve worshipped God by making an altar to Him. They made the altar from stones, and they brought only their best offerings to the altar. Adam and Eve taught Cain and Abel to make offerings to God, too.

On one offering day, Abel, the shepherd, chose a perfect lamb to bring to God. He had looked carefully at all his sheep. He wanted to give God the very best.

Cain, the farmer, also brought an offering to God. He took some of his fruit and grain, and brought it to the altar for God.

God was pleased with Abel's offering. He joyfully accepted the offering. But when God saw what Cain brought to Him, God was not pleased.

Cain pouted and said to his brother, "God likes you best."

God saw him pouting and asked, "Why are you pouting? All I want you to do is obey."

But Cain was still angry. He found Abel in the fields, caring for the flock. Cain then killed Abel because he was jealous of him. God punished Cain by sending him from his home and gardens.

God does not want us to be jealous of others. He wants us to be happy!

— Based on Genesis 4:1-16

Discussion Questions

1. Why was Cain jealous of his brother, Abel?

2. How should you feel when a friend gets a new bike or game?

craft

What You Need
- duplicated page
- crayons
- glue
- cotton balls
- magnet strips

What to Do
1. Duplicate and cut out one set of pictures for each child.
2. Allow the children to color the pictures.
3. Give each child a stretched cotton ball to glue to Abel's lamb.
4. Help the children tape their cutouts back-to-back.
5. Assist each child in sticking half of a 1" magnet to the back of each garment, making sure the magnets will meet when they are placed on either side of the cutouts.

What to Say
Make a cutout set to use in telling the Bible story. Retell the story, allowing the children to use their cutouts to act out the story.

Happy

Cain and Abel Cutouts

Follow the Motions

Abel

In your anger
do not sin.
Ephesians 4:26

Abel looked at his sheep
One, Two, Three.
He wanted his offering to God
To be the best that it could be!

Cain looked at his veggies,
Peas, beans and corn.
But God liked Abel's offering,
Oh, if his brother had not
been born!

Cain frowned at his brother,
He hated him, you see.
Then he killed brother Abel,
All because of his jealousy.

What You Need
• duplicated page
• crayons

What to Do
1. Duplicate a maze for each child.
2. Read the poem.
3. Give each child a maze and a crayon.
4. Say, "Your crayon is going on a journey. Everyone start with Abel, then go to each picture when I say it. You will end up at our memory verse, in the Bible."
5. Re-read the poem while the children complete the maze. Then read the memory verse, encouraging the children to repeat it with you.
6. To use the sheets more than once, cover them first in clear, self-stick plastic. When the children are finished, simply wipe off the crayon marks.

Puzzle answer key is on page 87

Happy

Fruity Smiles

snack

What You Need
• duplicated page
• banana slices
• cherries
• green grapes
• clear self-stick
  plastic
• crayons
• milk or juice
• small cups

What to Do
1. Duplicate a Smile
   Mat for each child.
2. Allow the children
   to color the fruit on
   their mats.
3. Go around and
   cover each mat
   with clear, self-
   stick plastic.
4. Instruct the
   children to make
   smiles from fruit
   by using the fruit
   illustrations on
   their mats: grapes
   for eyes, a cherry
   nose and banana
   slices for a mouth.
5. After everyone has
   completed his or her
   smile, pray the
   prayer on the mat.
6. Allow the children
   to eat their smiles.
   Offer small cups of
   milk or juice.

Happy

and friends that are sunny.

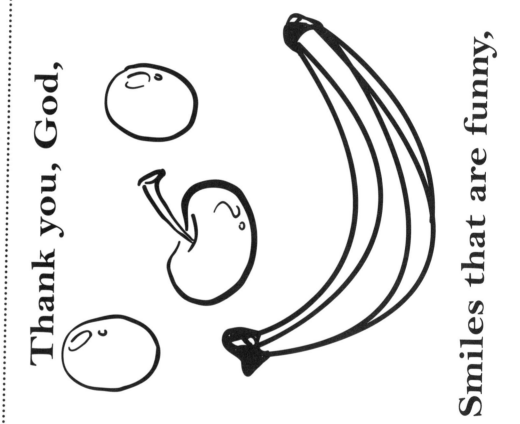

Thank you, God,

Smiles that are funny,

For good fruit for my tummy,

Smile or Frown

What To Say

Josh told Timmy he liked his new red ball.

Carrie poured Destiny's new bubbles out on the ground.

Ethan smiled when he saw Casey's new blue bike.

Chelsea gave Bailey a shiny gold star to wear when she won the race.

Zeke told Katie her new skates were ugly.

Happy

craft

What You Need

- duplicated page
- sandpaper
- white paper
- black construction paper
- crayons
- scissors
- glue

What to Do

1. Before class, remove the wrappers from the crayons. Trace the fruit and vegetables on sandpaper and cut them out. Also cut each fruit and vegetable from white paper for each child.

2. Show how to lay the paper fruit and vegetables on the same shapes of sandpaper and rub the crayon over the paper.

3. Allow the children to glue the platter, fruit and vegetables to the black paper.

Happy

Textured Fruit and Vegetable Platter

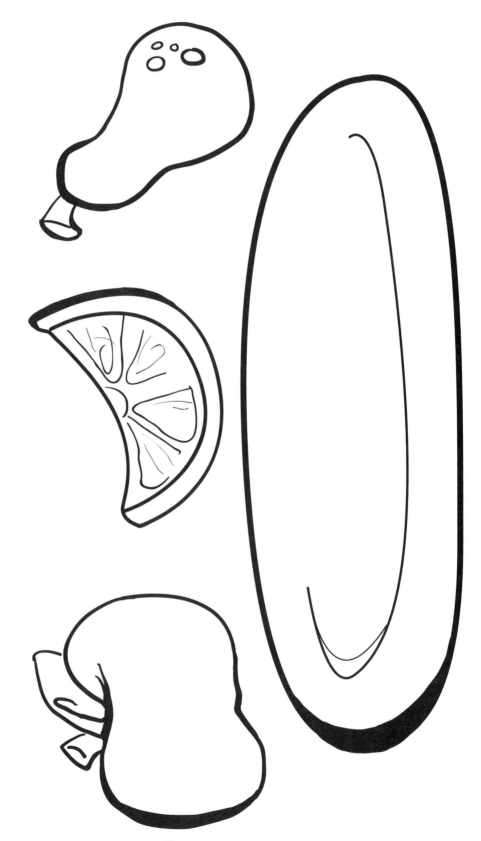

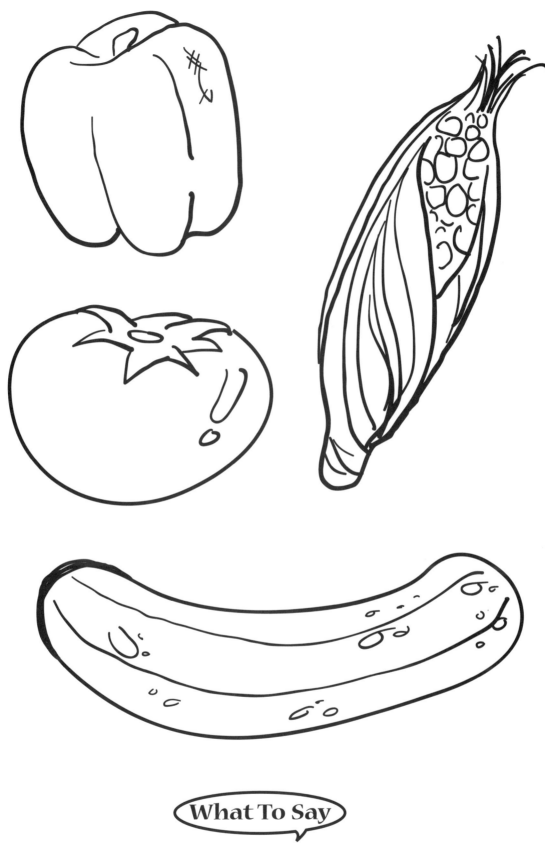

What To Say

Who brought the vegetables to God? (Cain)
Did God say to bring food to Him? (no)
Who brought a good offering to God? (Abel)
What was it? (a perfect lamb)

The Best Lamb Worksheet

What You Need
- duplicated page
- crayons
- cotton balls
- glue

What to Do
1. Before class, duplicate the activity sheet for each child.
2. Say, "Abel chose the best lamb to give to God. Can you find the lamb without a mark?"
3. Instruct the children to glue cotton to the unblemished lamb.
4. Allow the children to color their pictures.

What to Say
When we give offerings to God, He wants our best, too. He wants us to give Him ourselves. We need to eat good food, exercise our bodies and get plenty of sleep. Then we can give Him our best.

Happy

14

The "Happy" Song

I find it easy to be happy,
Be happy, be happy.
I find it easy to be happy,
For friends everywhere.

When (Josh) gets a (red ball),
A (red ball), a (red ball),
When (Josh) gets a (red ball),
I'll smile just for him.

No frowns will wiggle in,
Wiggle in, wiggle in.
No frowns will wiggle in,
I'll chase them away!

song

What You Need
• duplicated page
• smile and frown
  sign from page 11
• small toys

What to Do
1. Sing the song to the tune of "When We All Work Together."
2. Hold up the smile and frown sign during the song.
3. Substitute each child's name in the second verse as well as his or her favorite toy.
4. You can bring small toys from home so each child can select one to hold while you sing the song. If Kent is holding a green car sing, "When Kent gets a green car…"
5. You also can use the smile and frown signs for other times during class, such as when a child is pouting or feeling left out. Simply hold up the frown until the child smiles!

Happy

activity

What You Need
• duplicated page
• crayons

What to Do
1. Before class, duplicate the worksheet for each child.
2. Instruct the children to point to the pictures as you do. Point to the storybook and retell the story. Point to the children singing and sing, "Jesus Loves Me". Point to the children praying and pray a short praise prayer. Point to the Bible and repeat the memory verse. Have the boys point to the boy at the bottom and the girls point to the girl. Instruct the children to say, "We will worship God with our best."
3. Allow the children to color their pictures.

Happy

Worship Worksheet

What To Say

Both Abel and Cain wanted to worship God. Abel took his best. Cain brought an offering that didn't please God. Let's give God our best!

Chapter 2
God Wants Me to Be Joyful, not Grumbly

Memory Verse

Do everything without complaining.
Philippians 2:14

Story to Share
Grumble, Grumble, Grumble

The Israelites were joyful when God helped Moses lead them from slavery in Egypt. They sang songs and danced, and they were thankful that they were safe.

The Israelites weren't sure which way to travel as they left Egypt. But God had a plan for them. He had a special place He wanted them to go. So He gave them a cloud to follow.

After travelling for about three days, the Israelites were tired and thirsty. They had been walking for three days without any water to drink. Then some people in the front of the crowd saw springs of water ahead of them. The Israelites were so excited!

But as they drew closer and actually tasted the water, they found it was bitter. They could not drink this water after all. Now the Israelites were disappointed.

"I'm so thirsty," said one.

"Moses, why did you bring us out into the desert to die of thirst?" another asked with anger. "You should have left us in Egypt."

Soon all the people could think about was their thirst and hunger. They grumbled about everything! They had forgotten completely about God's miracle of helping them leave slavery in Egypt. More importantly, they forgot God's promise that He would always care for them.

Moses prayed and asked God what he should do with all these grumbly people.

God was not pleased with the Israelites' grumbles, but He helped them anyway.

"Throw a piece of wood into the water, Moses," said God. "The water will turn sweet, and the people can drink it."

Moses obeyed God and the water became sweet. The Israelites were happy as they drank it.

Moses told the people, "God does not like to hear grumbling. He will always take care of us."

— Based on Exodus 15:22-27

Discussion Questions

1. Why were the Israelites grumbling?
2. What do you grumble about? What does God think of grumbling?

activity

What You Need

- story pictures
- cotton balls
- magnets or hook and loop tape
- small piece of wood
- zipper-type sandwich bags
- crayons

What to Do

1. Duplicate and color the story pictures.
2. Glue cotton balls to the cloud pillar.
3. Attach magnets (or hook and loop tape if using a flannel board) to the back of the pictures and small piece of wood.
4. Tell the Bible story using the props. You also can give each child a set of pictures to color and take home. Provide zipper-type sandwich bags for the children to carry the pictures.

Joyful

Frown and Smile

Frown, smile,
Frown, then smile.
Frown, smile.
Frown, then smile.
Which should it be?
    (Hold out your hands
    with palms up.)
God wants us to have joyful
    hearts.
    (Smile and point
    at chest (heart).)
So it's a smile for me!
    (Do a jumping jack.)

game

What You Need
• duplicate page

What to Do
1. Duplicate a smile for each child.
2. Before class, hide the smiles around the room.
3. Repeat the action rhyme several times, doing the motions. Then instruct the children to hunt for a smile when you say, "So it's a smile for me!"
4. Instruct the children to draw on the backs of their smiles what makes them happy.

What to Say
Sometimes things go wrong and we just don't want to smile. God says to think of good things, and then a smile will come.

Joyful

19

bulletin board

What You Need

- duplicated page
- card stock, white, green and yellow
- poster paper, blue and brown
- colored cereals
- glue in small pots
- paint brushes
- green construction paper
- lettering or stencils (optional)

What to Do

1. Duplicate the flower to white card stock, the leaf to green card stock, and the smile to yellow card stock and cut them out, one set per child. Duplicate extra smiles. Tack blue poster paper along the top of a bulletin board, using about two-thirds of the space, then tack brown along the bottom. Use lettering, stencils or your freehand talent to write "Our Garden of Smiles" along the

Continued on next page...

Joyful

Garden of Smiles

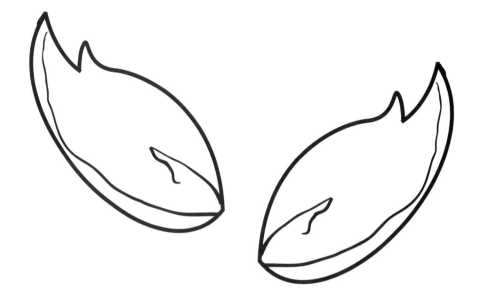

When a child is grumpy, take him or her to the board and say, "Your name is here in our Garden of Smiles. You must have forgotten yours today!" Take a smile off the board and give it to the child to place in his or her pocket.

Continued from previous page...

top of the board. Write the memory verse on the board.

2. Give each child a paint brush and glue. Instruct the children to brush glue on one petal of their flowers, then sprinkle it with cereal. Continue with each petal.

3. Print the name of each child on his or her leaf.

4. Instruct the children to glue their smiles to the middles of their flowers.

5. Post strips of green construction paper on the board (for stems), then attach each child's flower and leaf to one, varying the heights.

6. Attach the extra smiles along the bottom of the board.

Joyful

My Prayer Book

craft

What You Need
- duplicated page
- card stock
- stickers: food, animals, hearts, toys, etc.
- crayons
- stapler

What to Do
1. Duplicate the pattern to card stock once and to regular paper twice for each child.
2. Cut out the patterns (discard the top halves of the paper copies). Tape the first bottom half on the right side of the full piece. Tape the second one on the left side.
3. Allow the children to color the pictures in their books, finishing the faces to look like them.
4. Assist the children in choosing stickers for the things for which they want to thank God.

Joyful

Thank You God for

What To Say

Ask each child to close his or her book. Begin to pray, "We thank You, God, for all the joy You give to us. We thank You for…"

Go around the room and allow each child to say what is on the first page of his or her book.

Say, "We thank You for all these blessings and many more. Amen."

Smile S'mores

What You Need
- duplicated page
- colored card stock
- smiley face stickers
- clear, self-stick plastic
- chocolate graham crackers
- marshmallow cream
- candy-coated chocolate pieces

What to Do
1. Duplicate a smile mat to colored card stock for each child.
2. Allow the children to put one smiley face sticker in each scallop of their mats. Go around and cover the mats with clear plastic.
3. Give each child a graham cracker square spread with marshmallow cream, and a handful of candy pieces.
4. Allow the children to make smiley faces on their S'mores with the candy pieces.
5. Offer a prayer, then let the children enjoy their snacks.

Don't be grumpy–
Smile S'more!

Do everything without
complaining.
Philippians 2:14

Joyful

Sunshine Smile Straws

What You Need
- duplicated page
- red card stock
- 1 gallon lemonade
- 3 cups pineapple juice
- 2 cups lemon-lime soda
- plastic drinking straws
- glue

What to Do
1. Duplicate the mouth to red card stock and the teeth to white card stock for each child.
2. Have the children glue the teeth to the mouths.
3. Go around and punch a hole in the middle of the teeth.
4. Show how to insert a straw through the hole.
5. Have the children make Smile S'more snacks, page 23, to eat with their Smile Straws beverages.

What to Say
It's hard to be grumbly when we're thanking God!

Joyful

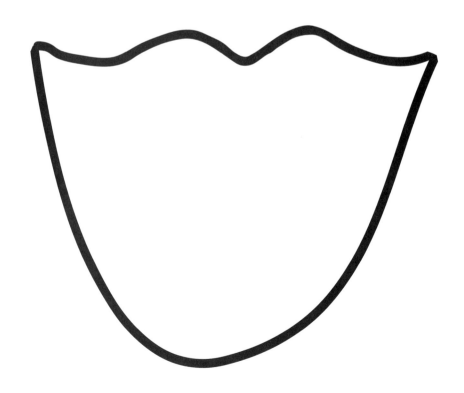

Tub of Joy

craft

What You Need
- duplicated page
- yellow paper
- safety scissors
- empty frosting tubs
- crayons
- glue
- scissors

What to Do
1. Duplicate a story wrap for each child. Duplicate 10 smiles to yellow paper for each child.
2. Allow the children to color the story wrap and glue it around an frosting tub.
3. Have each child cut out 10 smiles to place in his or her tub.

What to Say
When you are having trouble with the grumbles, hold your tub and remember the story of the grumbling Israelites. Then take a smile out and ask Jesus to take your grumbles away!

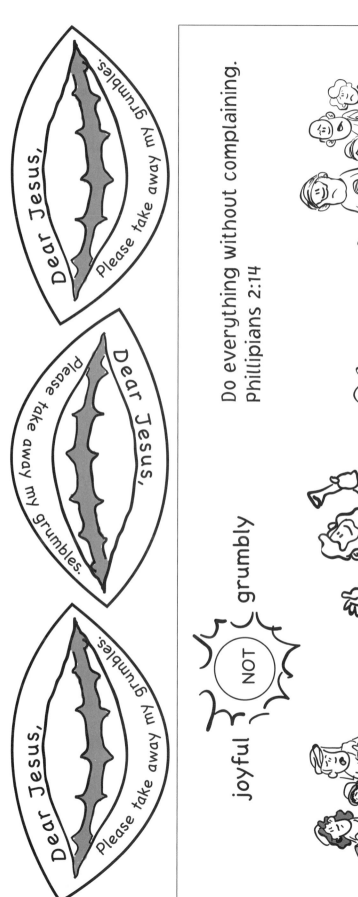

Dear Jesus, Please take away my grumbles.

Dear Jesus, Please take away my grumbles.

Dear Jesus, Please take away my grumbles.

Do everything without complaining. Philippians 2:14

joyful NOT grumbly

Joyful

Worksheet Match

What You Need
- duplicated page
- pencils

What to Do
1. Duplicate a worksheet for each child.
2. Discuss the first picture. Say, "The boy is supposed to put his game away. What should he do?" Instruct the children to draw a line from the boy to the game on the shelf and say, "Do everything without complaining."
3. Discuss each picture as the children match the pictures and say the memory verse.

What to Say
Do your parents ask you to do chores? What kinds of chores? (Allow time for the children to discuss chores.) What should we do when asked to do a chore? (Do everything without complaining.)

Joyful

Chapter 3
God Wants Me to Be Obedient, Not Disobedient

📖 Memory Verse

I have promised to obey your words.
Psalm 119:57

📖 Story to Share
I'll Do What I Want

Eli the high priest had two sons, Hophni and Phinehas, who were greedy and selfish. They did not show respect for God's House or for their father, Eli.

One day Eli told his sons that they needed to ask God to forgive them for their bad behavior.

"No, I just want to do what I want," said Hophni.

"Me, too," Phinehas agreed.

Unlike Hophni and Phineas, Samuel was a good helper to Eli. God had blessed Samuel's mother, Hannah, so she raised Samuel to love God. When Samuel was old enough, she took him to Eli. There were many chores Samuel could do for Eli, such as sweeping the floor and filling the lamps with oil.

Eli loved Samuel. He often would tell Samuel stories about God.

One night Samuel woke up to hear, "Samuel, Samuel." Samuel quickly got up and ran to Eli.

"I did not call you, Samuel," Eli told him. "Go back to sleep."

Then it happened a second time: "Samuel, Samuel," he heard. But Eli again said it wasn't him. When Samuel went to Eli the third time, the priest knew who was calling Samuel.

"If you hear your name again," said Eli, "say, 'Speak, Lord, for Your servant is listening.'"

When Samuel heard his name again, he answered, "Speak, Lord, for Your servant is listening."

God then told Samuel to tell Eli that his sons were evil: "They have cursed Me and disobeyed my commands. They will be punished."

The next morning Samuel told Eli what God had said to him. "The Lord is right," Eli said. "My sons have sinned and I did not stop them. If only they would have obeyed God rather than doing what they wanted."

Hophni and Phinehas were killed in a battle with the Philistines. They were punished for their disobedience.

— Based on 1 Samuel 3:1-19

❓ Discussion Questions

1. What did Hophni and Phinehas tell Eli when Eli asked them to obey God?
2. What should you do when your parents ask you to obey?

Counting 1, 2, 3

How many Samuels lived with Eli?	How many sons did Eli have?	How many times did Samuel go to Eli in the night?

Erase-a-Smile

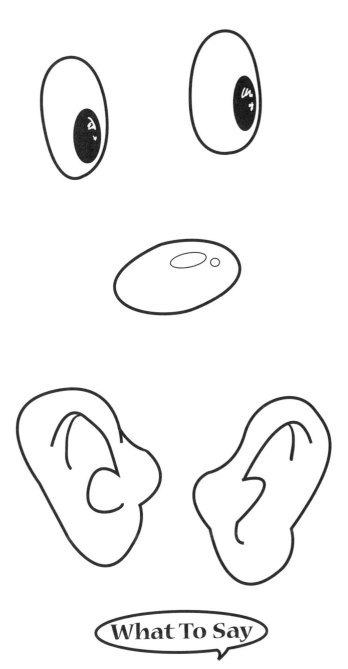

craft

What You Need
- duplicated page
- zipper-type sandwich bags
- duct tape
- tempera paint in skin tones (pink, peach, brown, tan)
- crayons
- glue

What to Do
1. Duplicate and cut out a set of face features for each child. Partially fill a sandwich bag with paint for each child. Push the air out of each bag, then secure with duct tape.
2. Give each child a pre-filled bag of paint.
3. Allow the children to color and glue the face features to their paint bags.
4. Read the statements. Tell the children to use their fingers to draw smiles on their faces if the child is obedient. Tell the children to draw frowns if the child is not obedient.

What To Say

Mommy told Jacob to pick up his blocks. Jacob looked at a book instead. (frown)

Carli's mother told her not to eat a cookie before dinner. Carli put the spoons on the table instead. (smile)

Daddy told Carson to jump into bed. Carson pulled the covers over his head. (smile)

When Brandon asked to use Daddy's knife, he said no. Brandon picked up the knife and cut his finger. (frown)

The Bible says, "Don't tell a lie." Elena told her mother the truth when she broke a glass plate. (smile)

Shawn said, "Don't touch the paint." Dustin got too close and got paint on his fingers. (frown)

Obedient

Ice Cream Cone Treat

snack

What You Need
- duplicated page
- rubber bands
- 8" x 8" fabric squares in ice cream colors
- small treats (candy, erasers, coins, etc.)

What to Do
1. Duplicate a cone and cut a fabric square for each child.
2. Assist the children in rolling the cone shapes and gluing the overlapped edges together.
3. Give each child a fabric square and some small treats. Help each child pull the fabric up and around the treats and fasten the fabric with rubber bands.
4. Help each child run a rim of glue around the top of his or her cone and press the "ice cream" into the glue, rubber band side down.

What to Say
Your cone is filled with treats, but can you obediently wait until you get home to open it?

Obedient

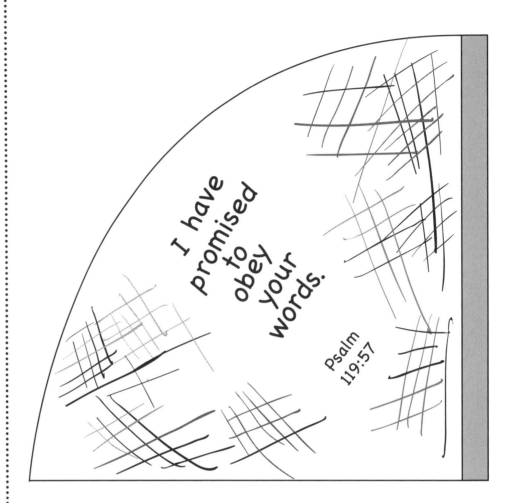

I have promised to obey your words.

Psalm 119:57

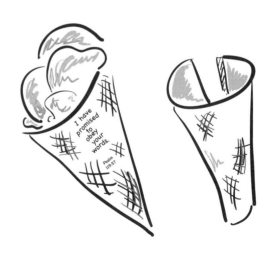

Obedience Lesson

What You Need
- duplicated page
- crayons

What to Do
1. Duplicate the pictures to card stock and cut out the pictures.
2. Lay out the pictures for early children to color.
3. Hold up each picture and discuss obeying that person.
4. After the pictures have been discussed, hold up the question mark. Ask, "Do you have trouble being obedient?"
5. Pray together, asking God to help the children to be obedient.

What to Say
Our verse says, "I have promised to obey your words." Whom does the Bible tell us to obey?

Obedient

"Obedience" Song

song

What You Need
- duplicated page
- black construction paper
- red ribbons
- glue
- letter stickers
- gold cross stickers

What to Do
1. Trace the larger Bible pattern on black construction paper and cut out one for each child. Also duplicate the smaller Bible pages on white paper.
2. Allow the students to glue the Bible page to the cover and fold it in half.
3. Help each child glue a ribbon down the center.
4. Help the children spell "Bible" with gold stickers on the front of their Bible and stick a cross underneath.
5. Sing the song to the tune of "Ten Little Indians." Instruct the children to hold up their new Bibles for the first verse, then open their

Continued at right...

Obedient

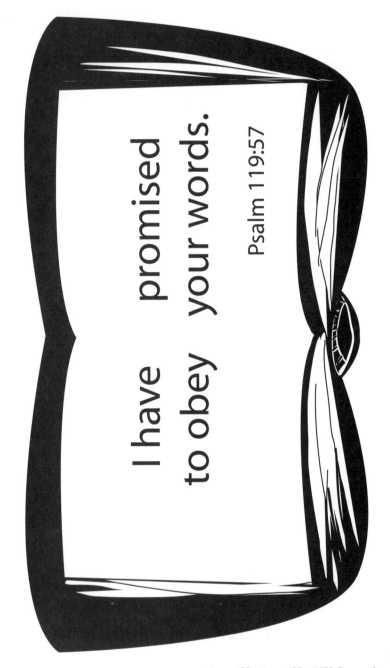

I have promised to obey your words.

Psalm 119:57

Continued from left...
Bibles for the second and third verses.

What to Say
Eli's sons were not obedient. God was not happy with their disobedience. God wants us to obey His laws.

I will, I will, I'll be obedient.
I will, I will, I'll be obedient.
I will, I will, I'll be obedient.
I will obey God's Word.

I will, I will, I'll be obedient.
I will, I will, I'll be obedient.
I will, I will, I'll be obedient.
I will obey my Mom. (Dad)

"O"bedience Story Visuals

game
· · · · · · · · · · · ·

What You Need
• duplicated page
• crayons or markers
• hook and loop tape

What to Do
1. Cut out and color the four visuals (or copy them on colored paper).
2. Attach the hook and loop tape to the back of each picture.
3. Say, "The first letter of "obedience" is "O." Write the letter on the board. Can you make an "O" with your mouth?" After they make O's with their mouths, have the children make O's with their thumbs and first fingers, and then with their arms.
4. Tell the Bible story with the pictures, placing them on the board to form an "O." After you tell the story, remove the picture of the disobedient boys.

Continued on next page...

What To Say

What happens when we take the disobedient boys out of the "O"? It ruins the "O"! Even a little bit of disobedience can ruin your life. God wants you to obey.

Obedient

33

Obedient Me!

game
. . . .

What You Need
- duplicated page
- decorated bag

What to Do
1. Duplicate and cut out the body parts. Place the parts in a bag.
2. Invite a child to put his or her hand in the bag and pull out a part.
3. Have the child tell how that body part can show obedience (e.g., ear: We can listen to our teacher tell about Jesus; hand: We can pick up our toys when play time is over)

What to Say
Sometimes our mouths say, "I will obey," but our other body parts don't do what they should. Let's get all our parts to be obedient.

Obedient

Samuel's Robe Mobile

craft

What You Need
- duplicated page
- poster board
- crayons
- yarn

What to Do

1. Duplicate and cut out a robe for each child. Create a mobile bar from two strips of poster board. Punch holes on the mobile bar, as shown in the diagram. Tie a length of yarn to the top of the bar for hanging.
2. Say, "When Samuel went to live in the temple, his mommy brought him a new robe every year."
3. Give each child a robe and instruct the children to color their robes with their favorite colors.
4. Explain to the children that they can help you make a colorful mobile for your classroom.
5. As each child brings you a

Continued at right...

Obedient

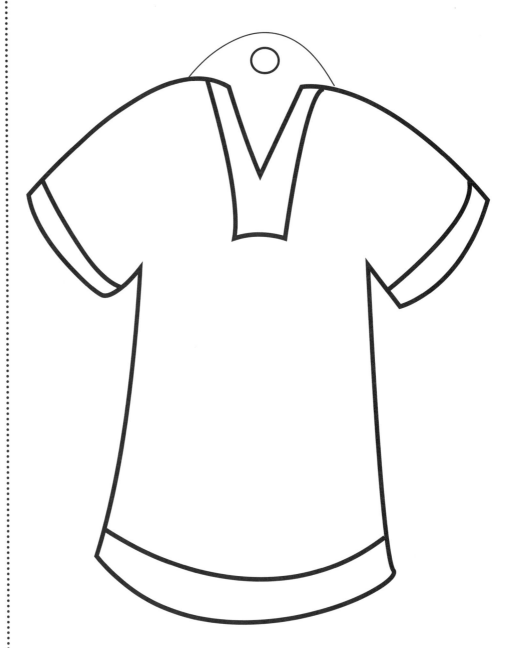

Continued from left...
colored robe write his or her name on the back and say, "Just like Samuel, (Justin) will be following God, obediently."

6. Punch a hole in the neck of each robe and tie a piece of yarn to the hole. Tie the free ends of the yarn to the mobile bar's holes, varying the lengths.
7. Hang the mobile where the children can enjoy it. Reinforce the lesson by showing each child's robe and saying, "(Justin) promises to be obedient."

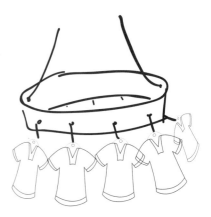

Chapter 4
God Wants Me to Be Timely, Not Tardy

Memory Verse

Be ready to do whatever is good.
Titus 3:1

Story to Share
Five Tardy Girls

One day Jesus told a story about 10 bridesmaids. Each bridesmaid had a lamp. The bridesmaids were waiting for the groom so they could light his way to the bride's house for the wedding.

The groom took a long time to get ready. Five of the bridesmaids planned ahead and brought extra oil for their lamps.

"Where's your extra oil?" one bridesmaid asked the five who did not bring extra.

"Oh, the bridegroom will probably come before we need more," one replied.

"If not, we can always go get more," another said.

"What if you're late?" asked the first bridesmaid.

"Oh, the bridegroom won't care. We'll still get there," they answered.

But the bridegroom took even longer than they thought. It got so late, the bridesmaids fell asleep.

Then they heard, "The bridegroom is coming! The bridegroom is coming!"

Quickly, the bridesmaids jumped to their feet. They straightened their dresses and tried to light their lamps. But they had left the lamps lit while they slept, and now the oil in the lamps was gone.

The five bridesmaids who brought extra oil began pouring it into their lamps. Those without extra oil knew they were going to miss the bridegroom.

"We'll just run and get some extra oil and be right back," they said.

But by the time they got back from getting the oil, the bridegroom had met his bride and together with the bridesmaids ahead of them to light the way, went to the bridegroom's house for the seven-day feast. The bridegroom locked the door after everyone entered and the festivities began.

The tardy bridesmaids knocked on the door when they arrived, but no one would open the door for them. They couldn't enter the celebration. Only those on time were able to join in the eating, singing and dancing.

Jesus told this story to warn us to be ready for heaven. When we are always ready to do what is good each day, we also will be ready for heaven.

— Based on Matthew 25:6-12

Discussion Questions

1. How could the tardy bridesmaids have planned better?
2. What are some things you can do to make sure you aren't a tardy boy or girl?

song

What You Need
• duplicated page
• yellow paper
• craft sticks
• glue

What to Do
1. Duplicate the hive and bee on yellow paper and cut out a set for each child. Cut a ½" slit on the dashed lines at the top of the hive.
2. Give each child a hive, a bee and a craft stick.
3. Show how to fold the hive in half at the top, fold in the tabs and glue them together at the bottom so the hive stands.
4. Instruct the children to glue their bees to the top ends of their craft sticks.
5. Show how to insert the craft stick into the top of the hive.
6. Sing the song to the tune of "Three Blind Mice" while the children "buzz" their bees around, ending up with the bees in the top of the hives.

Timely

Bee-ing Ready

Buzz, buzz, buzz.
Buzz, buzz, buzz.
I'll be on time.
I'll be on time.

Always ready to do
what is good,
Being on time like
God says I should.
Buzz, buzz, buzz.

Doing Good Worksheet

puzzle

What You Need
- duplicated page
- crayons

What to Do
1. Duplicate a worksheet for each child.
2. Say, "There are boys and girls on this sheet who are obeying our memory verse: 'Be ready to do what is good.'"
3. Instruct the children to color the pictures of the children who are doing good, and to draw a large "X" over the pictures of those who are not doing good.

What to Say
What should the girl throwing trash on the ground do instead? What about the boy throwing stones at the bird?
Look at the faces of the children doing good. Doing good makes us happy. It makes Jesus happy, too.

Timely

39

puzzle
. . . .

What You Need
• duplicated page
• envelopes
• stamps

What to Do
1. Duplicate a letter for each child. Personalize each letter with the child's name.
2. Cut out the lamp, then cut it apart so there is a puzzle piece for each child. (For larger groups, use two lamps.)
3. Address the envelopes, adding a puzzle piece to each one.
4. As each child arrives with his or her puzzle piece, tape it to the board.
5. After all have arrived, have the children group around the puzzle and hold hands.
6. Thank God for each child who is able to be in church and ask Him to help those who are unable to be there.

Timely

Ready to Do Good Invitation

Dear _____,

Come to church and help complete our puzzle. Our Bible lesson is about five kids who were ready to do good, and five kids who weren't. So be on time and bring your puzzle piece. We're going to have fun!

_____

Honey Roll-Ups

What You Need

- duplicated page
- toothpicks
- 8" tortillas
- 1 cup peanut butter
- ½ cup honey
- plastic knives or spoons
- bananas, peeled
- wax paper
- wet towelettes
- crayons

What to Do

1. Mix the peanut butter and honey.
2. Allow the children to color their bees.
3. Assist the children in folding their bees on the dashed lines and gluing a toothpick inside each one.
4. Give each child a tortilla and some peanut butter and honey.
5. Help the children spread the mixture on their tortillas.
6. Give each child a banana and demonstrate how to roll the banana in the tortilla.
7. Show how to stick the bee on top to hold the tortilla.

What To Say

Bee-ing healthy helps us to buzz around, ready to do what is right. God wants us to eat good foods. Good foods help us grow strong and healthy bodies. What other foods are good for us?

Timely

41

Little Lamp Play

craft

. . . .

What You Need
- duplicated page
- large heart stickers or red stamp pad and sponge heart
- crayons
- glue

What to Do
1. Duplicate and cut out a lamp card and poem for each child.
2. Fold the cards.
3. Let the children color their lamps.
4. Allow the children to glue the poems to the inside fronts of their cards.
5. Help the children put heart stickers or stamps inside their cards. Print each child's name in his or her heart.
6. Have the children hold up the fronts of their lamp cards while you say the first part of the poem. Then have them open the cards so the hearts show.
7. Pray, asking God to help each child be ready to obey the command to do what is right. Call each child by name.

Timely

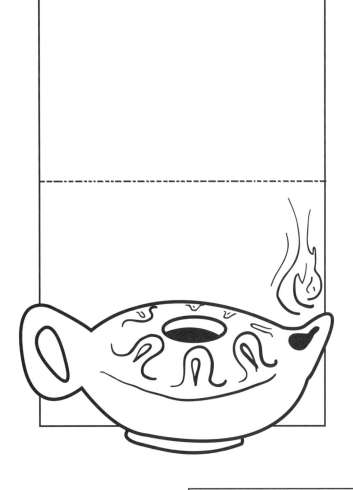

What To Say

Five of the bridesmaids brought extra oil for their lamps. They were ready. You can ask Jesus to help you be ready to do good, too.

Here's the bridesmaid's lamp
Lighting up the night.
She wants to keep it burning –
Burning nice and bright.

Here's my heart's lamp
Lighting up each day.
I want to keep it burning –
With the good I do and say.

On Time Clock

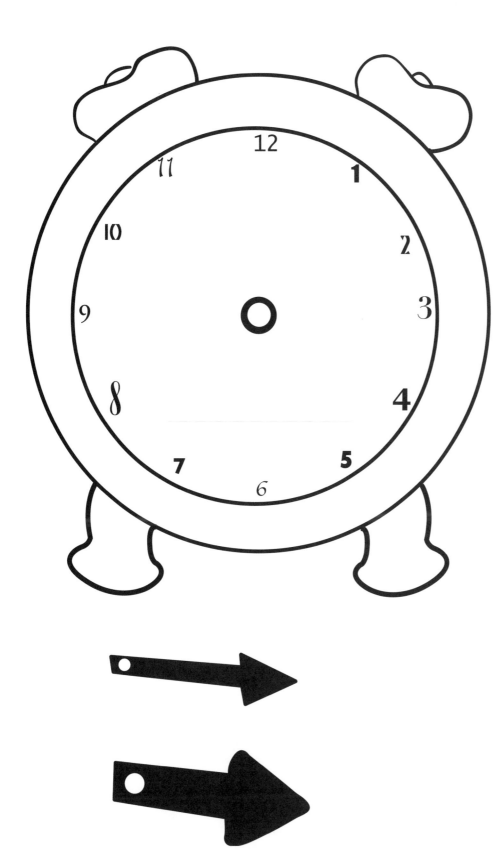

What You Need
• 10 duplicated pages
• paper fasteners

What to Do
1. Attach the hands to the clocks with paper fasteners.
2. Turn the hands on the first clock to 1:00 and print the first word of the verse ("Be") on the line. Put the second clock's hands at 2:00 and write the second word ("ready"). Continue to 10:00.
3. Tape the clocks to the floor, spacing them 6" apart.
4. Instruct the children to stand at the first clock.
5. One child jumps to the 1:00 clock and says the first word with you, jumps to the 2:00 clock and says the next word, and continues to the 10:00 clock.
7. When the child lands on the 10:00, the rest of the children should cheer and say, "(Olivia's) on time!"

Timely

Time to Read Book

What You Need
- duplicated page
- card stock
- crayons
- paper fasteners
- glue

What to Do
1. Duplicate a clock cover and hands to card stock for each child. Duplicate accordion pictures on regular paper for each child.
2. Before class, fold the clock covers on the dashed lines and attach the hands to the clocks with paper fasteners.
3. Allow the children to color the story pictures.
4. Assist the children in accordion-folding their story pictures.
5. Allow each child to glue the back of the first picture to the inside front of the cover, and the back of the last picture to the inside back, to hold in the pages.
6. Allow the children to take turns telling the story with the books.

Continued on next page...

Timely

44

Matthew 25:6-12

45

Timely Bulletin Board

What You Need
- duplicated pages
- colored paper
- stencil letters
- paper plate
- plastic knife, fork and spoon
- napkin
- game pieces
- crumpled colored paper

What to Do
1. Duplicate the clock to card stock and cut it out.
2. Duplicate the hands to colored paper, one set for each child.
3. Attach letters and the clock to the board, as shown.
4. Glue the plate, plastic ware and napkin to the board.
5. Attach the game pieces and the crumpled paper to the board.
6. Glue the clock hands together at different times: 1:00, 2:00, etc.
7. Print the name of each student on a

Continued on next two pages...

Timely

It's ⏰ to do Good!

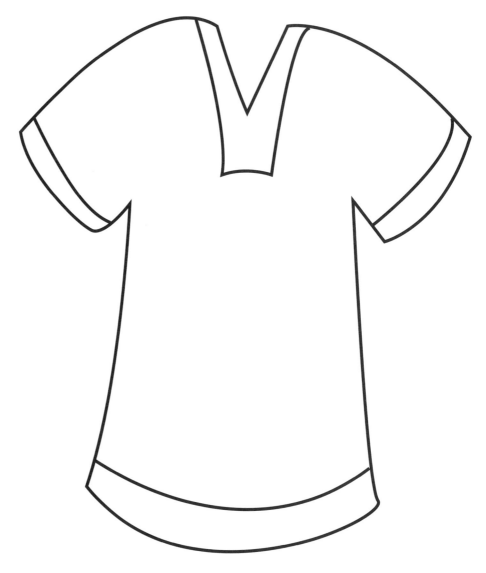

46

bulletin board
. . . .

Continued from previous page...

set of hands and attach to the board.

What to Say

Our memory verse tells us, "Be ready to do whatever is good." Our board shows us some good things we can do, such as set or clear off the table, put our dirty clothes in the hamper, put our games and toys away, or clean up our art mess. Can you think of other ways you can be helpful?

Continued on next page...

Timely

Chapter 5
God Wants Me to Be Honest, Not Deceitful

Memory Verse

Do not lie to each other.
Colossians 3:9

Story to Share
A Sneaky Twin

Esau and Jacob were twins. Esau was the oldest twin, so he would inherit their father's special blessing. This was a very big honor. Not only would the oldest son get many of his father's things when he died, but he also would be the leader of the family.

The two brothers were opposites. Esau was his father Isaac's favorite son. He liked to hunt in the woods.

Jacob was his mother, Rebekah's, favorite. He liked to stay near home.

Jacob knew that Esau would get their father's blessing. He wished that he had been born first. "Mother, why?" he would ask with a jealous heart. "Why can't Father give me the blessing?"

"Son," Rebekah would say, "you know the oldest son receives the blessing. But don't worry, I have a plan."

Rebekah and Jacob planned to trick his father, who was blind, into giving the blessing to Jacob instead of Esau. One day while Esau was out hunting deer for his father's dinner, Rebekah prepared a meal for Jacob to give to his father. Because Esau's arms were hairy and Jacob's were smooth, Rebekah took a goatskin and wrapped it around Jacob's arms.

The trick worked! When Isaac felt Jacob's hairy arms and smelled the delicious meat dish, he thought Jacob was Esau. So he gave Jacob the blessing.

Jacob took what wasn't his, because he was full of deceit instead of love for his brother. He later was punished for not being honest.

— Based on Genesis 27:1-20

Discussion Questions

1. Are you sometimes dishonest with other people?
2. What can you do to be honest and free of deceit?

song

....

What You Need
• sheet
• chair

What to Do

1. Practice the song before class so you know it.
2. Put a sheet over a chair to represent a tent.
3. Have the children hold hands and skip around the tent, singing the song to the tune of "All Around the Mulberry Bush."

Honest

All Around the Tent

All around the tent that day,
tent that day,
tent that day,
All around the tent that day,
Jacob was deceitful.

He showed his father hairy arms,
hairy arms,
hairy arms,
He showed his father hairy arms,
Oh that was against the rule!

(Spoken) Do not lie to each other!

God wants me to be honest,
honest,
honest,
God wants me to be honest,
And tell the truth always.

Learn your lesson from Jacob,
Jacob,
Jacob,
Learn your lesson from Jacob,
And watch what all you say.

(Spoken) Do not lie to each other!

Honest Answers Worksheet

Honest

puzzle

What You Need
• duplicated page
• crayons
• self-stick magnet strips, cut in ½" pieces

What to Do
1. Duplicate and cut out a story set for each child.
2. Allow the children to color the pictures.
3. Assist the children in attaching the magnet sections to the backs of Jacob and Esau and the fronts of the tent and woods.

What to Say
Jacob and Esau liked different things.
What did Jacob like?
(to stay close to the tent)
What did Esau like?
(to go hunting)
Can you get Jacob to stand by the tent and Esau to go hunting?

Honest

Jacob and Esau Cutouts

Sssssneaky Snake

What You Need
- duplicated page
- colored paper

What to Do
1. Duplicate the snake on colored paper and cut it out.
2. Instruct the children to sit in a circle. Play the game like "Duck, Duck, Goose."
3. Choose one child to be Jacob.
4. Jacob should sneak around the outside of the circle and drop the snake behind another child. When he does, he should say, "Sssssssnake!"
5. The child that is chosen should then stand up and try to catch the deceitful Jacob before he gets back to the empty place and sits down. The other child then becomes Jacob.

When Satan came to Eve, he came in the form of a snake. We sometimes say that someone is "as sneaky as a snake." We're going to play a game that will remind you to be honest instead of sneaky like Jacob was.

Honest

53

Twin Snacks

What You Need

- duplicated page
- tortillas
- table knife
- cream cheese
- shredded cheese
- paper fasteners
- crayons
- scissors

What to Do

1. Duplicate a Jacob, Esau and arm set for each child.
2. Allow the children to color the pictures.
3. Spread tortillas with cream cheese, using two tortillas per child. Allow each child to sprinkle shredded cheese "hair" on one tortilla.
4. Cut tortillas in half. Starting at one side, roll tortilla halves into "arms." Make two pairs of arms per child.
5. Have the children lay the smooth tortilla arms on Jacob and the hairy ones on Esau.
6. When the snack is finished, attach the paper arms to the pictures with paper fasteners.

Honest

What To Say

Say, "Just like Esau and Jacob were different, we are all different from each other. Each of us has to make the choice to be honest or dishonest. Let's ask Jesus to help us choose honesty." Pray a short prayer, naming each child, and ask that God help each one be honest.

Verse Signs

Do not lie
to each other.
Colossians 3:9

DO NOT
———
LIE

(What To Say)

Have you ever seen a sign along the road that said, "Do not enter"? If the person driving the car disobeyed the sign, he or she could have an accident. The sign is there for a reason. Our sign says, "Do not lie." God's command is for a purpose. If you disobey it, you will not be honest!

craft

. . . .

What You Need
- duplicated page
- bright yellow paper
- glue
- craft sticks
- safety scissors

What to Do
1. Duplicate the page to bright yellow paper for each child.
2. Allow the children to cut out the signs.
3. Show the children how to glue the front and back of a sign together. Show how to sandwich an end of a craft stick between the two pieces.
4. Have the children hold up their signs and say, "Do not lie." Then instruct them to turn the signs around and quote the verse.

Honest

puzzle

What You Need
- duplicated page
- red, blue, purple and green crayons

What to Do
1. Duplicate a worksheet for each child.
2. Read the "Who" questions and allow the children to answer the questions together.
3. Help the children use the correct colors to answer the questions.

What to Say
Who was the daddy of Jacob and Esau? Draw a circle around him with the green crayon.
Who was the mommy of Jacob and Esau? Draw a circle around her with the blue crayon.
Who was the brother who liked to hunt? Draw a circle around him with the red crayon.
Who was the sneaky brother? Draw a circle around him with a purple crayon.

Honest

Isaac

Jacob

Esau

Rebekah

Chapter 6
God Wants Me to Be Patient, Not Impatient

 Memory Verse

A man's wisdom gives him patience.
Proverbs 19:11

Story to Share
The Patient Brother

Joseph lived with his father, Jacob, in Canaan. Joseph had ten older brothers and one younger brother.

Because Jacob loved Joseph, he made him a colorful coat. Instead of being happy that Joseph had a beautiful new coat, his brothers became angry and jealous.

One morning Joseph told his brothers, "I had a dream last night. We were all tying bundles of grain in the fields. Suddenly, my bundle stood straight up, and your bundles bowed down to it."

When they heard about his dream, Joseph's brothers hated him even more. "We'll never bow down to you," they said.

Joseph was sad his brothers were angry with him. "When will my brothers show kindness to me?" he wondered. But Joseph was patient with his brothers. He knew God was in charge. Joseph's brothers hated him so much that they sold him as a slave into Egypt. Still, Joseph was patient.

As he lived in Egypt, Joseph never forgot his family. He longed to see his father and younger brother, Benjamin. But each time Joseph wondered "when," he reminded himself to be patient.

One day Joseph was made second in command to Pharaoh, the ruler of Egypt. Joseph was in charge of sharing food with hungry people.

Back in Canaan, Joseph's family did not have food. They heard there was food in Egypt, so they came to see Joseph. But they didn't realize he was their brother!

When Joseph's hungry brothers came to visit, they bowed down to him, just as the bundles of grain did in Joseph's dream. Then they recognized that this leader was their brother! They asked Joseph to forgive them for their anger and jealousy.

Joseph forgave his brothers. His brothers and their father moved so they could live near him. Joseph was glad he had been patient and waited for God's timing.

— Based on Genesis 37-50

Discussion Questions

1. Do you think it was hard for Joseph to wait to see his brothers love him?

2. Has your impatience ever caused you trouble?

Circle the Picture

puzzle

What You Need
- duplicated page
- crayons

What to Do
1. Duplicate a worksheet for each child.
2. Discuss each picture. Instruct the children to circle the pictures of the places where Joseph had to wait.
3. Allow the children to color their pictures of Joseph and his colorful coat.

What to Say
Joseph didn't have to wait on the playground, but you might have to wait your turn to go down the slide. Joseph didn't have to wait for the drinking fountain, but you might have to. And you might need to wait for your turn to use the craft supplies. You can learn to be patient – just like Joseph!

Patient

Handy Sign for "Wait"

What You Need
- duplicated page
- crayons

What to Do
1. Duplicate a sheet for each child.
2. Allow the children to trace the letters.
3. Teach the children the sign for "wait": wiggle the fingers of both hands with one hand in front of the other.
4. You can use this sign whenever a student becomes impatient. Without saying a word, you can suggest that he or she wait.

Patient

How Many Bundles?

puzzle

What You Need
- duplicated page
- necklace-length ribbons
- card stock
- crayons
- safety scissors
- glue
- hole punch

What to Do
1. Duplicate a sheet for each child.
2. Cut a 3" circle out of card stock for each child. Punch holes in the tops. Thread one ribbon through each hole and tie the ends.
3. Ask the children to count the bundles in the first row.
4. Repeat the question for the other rows.
5. Count all the bent bundles with the children. Ask them how many older brothers Joseph had.
6. Assist each child in cutting out the one standing bundle.
7. Allow the students to color and glue the standing bundles to the medallion necklaces.

Patient

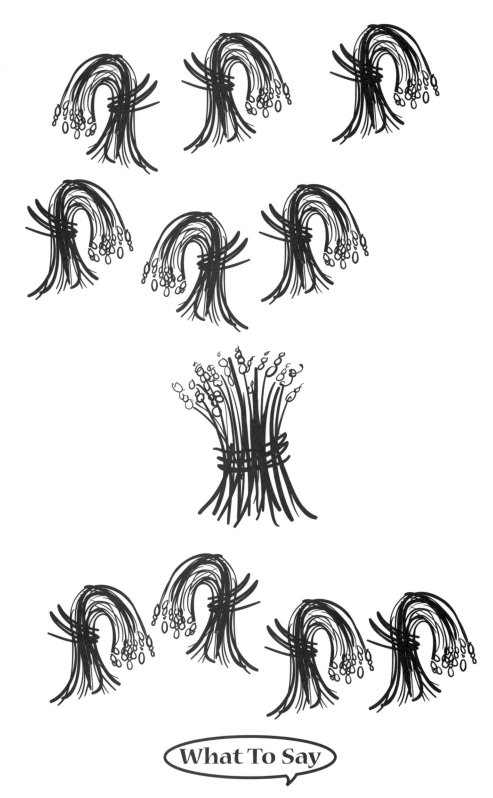

What To Say

Joseph had a dream that 10 bundles bowed down to his bundle. He had to be patient and wait for that day to come. Do you have trouble waiting when you mother says, "Just a minute"? Your teacher will help you make a medal to wear to remind you to be patient.

"If You're Wise" Song

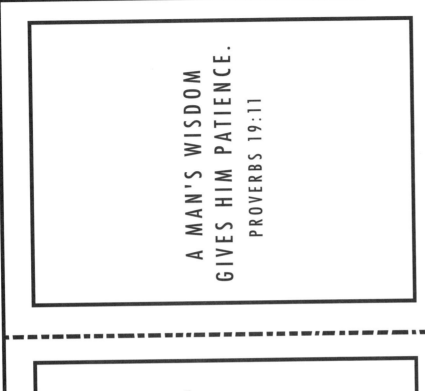

A MAN'S WISDOM
GIVES HIM PATIENCE.
PROVERBS 19:11

WAIT

song

What You Need
• duplicated page
• jumbo craft sticks
• crayons

What to Do
1. Duplicate a "wait" sign for each child.
2. Allow the children to color their signs.
3. Assist each child in folding his or her sign on the dashed lines and gluing it together with the top of a craft stick sandwiched between.
4. Sing the song to the tune of "If You're Happy and You Know It."

What to Say
You'll have to use your patience to sing this song – hold your "wait" sign in your lap until we say, "Wait."

If you're wise and you know it, then you'll wait.
(spoken: We'll wait!)
If you're wise and you know it, then you'll wait.
(spoken: We'll wait!)
If you're wise and you know it,
then you'll be a patient person.
If you're wise and you know it, then you'll wait.
(spoken: We'll wait!)

Patient

61

Joseph's Apple Holes

snack

What You Need
- duplicated page
- crayons
- clear, self-stick plastic
- apples
- lemon juice
- peanut butter or apple butter
- raisins

What to Do
1. Duplicate an apple placemat for each child.
2. Peel and cut the apples in half. Core them and scoop out the seeds. To prevent browning, dip the cut apples in lemon juice.
3. Fill the holes in the apples with peanut butter and raisins. For students with peanut allergies, fill the holes with apple butter.
4. Give each child an apple placemat to color. Assist in printing each child's name on the leaf.
5. Go around and cover each apple placemat with clear plastic.

Patient

A man's wisdom gives him patience.
Proverbs 19:11

What To Say

As the children arrive, show them what their snack will be. Throughout the session, mention the apples filled with peanut butter and raisins. When it's time to eat, ask, "Was it difficult for you to wait for Joseph's Apple Holes? Sometimes when we want something it's hard to be patient. Joseph learned to be patient at home, in a dark hole and even in a prison cell."

Joseph's Storyboard

What You Need
- duplicated page
- poster board
- crayons
- glue
- craft knife

What to Do
1. Duplicate a storyboard and Joseph figure for each child.
2. Instruct the children to color the storyboards and figures.
3. Allow the children to glue their storyboards to poster board.
4. Assist the children in cutting out the Joseph figures.
5. Using the craft knife (away from the reach of the children), cut slits on the storyboards where indicated.

A man's wisdom gives him patience. Proverbs 19:11

What To Say

Say, "Let's see all the opportunities Joseph had to be patient. Push Joseph's tab in the first slit. When was Joseph patient?" Continue with the other slits until the last one, then say the memory verse with the children.

Patient

Just Like Joseph

bulletin board

What You Need
- duplicated page
- card stock
- crayons
- clear, self-stick plastic
- self-stick hook and loop tape
- colorful border
- lettering
- pictures of children (optional)

What to Do
1. Duplicate a page on card stock for each child. Cut off the ponytails for boys. Give each child a Patient Kid to color. Assist the child in printing his or her name on the lines.
2. If you want to use real pictures of the children in your class, carefully cut the faces from the pictures and glue them over the Patient Kids' faces.
3. Cover each Patient Kid with clear, self-stick plastic.
4. Attach a colorful border to the

Continued on next page...

Patient

Continued from previous page...

bulletin board. Attach lettering that says "Just like Joseph" to the top of the board (or write by hand). Attach lettering that says "We'll wait our turn!" to the bottom of the board.

5. Cut hook and loop tape into squares. Press one side of the square onto the back of each Patient Kid. Press the other side in a line on the bulletin board.

6. Use the board as an "I'm first" board. The first one in line gets to be first at whatever activity is next. Then that student's Patient Kid will go to the back of the line and the next one will be first for the next activity. As that one goes first, encourage those in line to say, "I'll be patient."

Just Like Joseph

Nicholas   Brandon   Ashley   Kayla   Anthony   Isabella

We'll wait our turn!

Patient

What You Need
• duplicated page

What to Do
1. Duplicate a page for each child.
2. Say the poem while showing the children the motions.
3. Give each child a copy of the finger play to take home.

Patient

Patient Joseph

Joseph was only one,
   (hold up one finger)
His older brothers numbered 10.
   (hold up 10 fingers)
He wanted to be their friend,
He could only wonder "when."

He was thrown in a pit,
   (make circle with left
   arm/poke right hand inside)
Sold to Egyptians as a slave.

Oh how hard it was for him to
   wait, (tap watch)
To wait and to be brave.

But then the day did come,
   (nod head)
When they saw him as their
   friend.
He was glad that he was patient,
   (bow)
And their hatred found an end.

Chapter 7
God Wants Me to Be Respectful, Not Rebellious

Memory Verse

Submit yourselves...to every authority.
1 Peter 2:13

Story to Share
You Can't Make Me

King David's son, Absalom, was a very handsome man. But he also had a disobedient heart. He did not show respect to his father, and he rebelled against God's law. David loved his son, but Absalom had a wicked heart.

Absalom planned a way to become king instead of David. Early in the morning, he rode into the city in his shiny chariot. He wanted to talk to the people who were coming to see the king.

"King David is too busy to see you," Absalom lied, "but if I were king I would take care of your problems."

One day Absalom told his father he was going to Hebron to worship God, but he was lying. When he arrived in Hebron, he told the people there that he had become king. Many of the people who had become his friends joined his army.

King David soon found out what Absalom had done. He was sad that the son he loved had plotted to take the kingdom from him.

David gathered together an army to fight against Absalom's army. As the soldiers were leaving to fight, David told them, "I know this battle must be fought, but my heart hurts when I think of my son. Watch out for him. I love him even though he has done this evil thing."

David's army fought hard and won a great victory. Thousands of Absalom's soldiers were killed. Absalom saw that he had lost the battle, so he jumped on his mule to run away.

The mule galloped under a tree with low branches. Absalom's hair caught in a branch and he was left hanging there when the mule kept running. Absalom died hanging from that tree.

When a messenger arrived with the news of Absalom's death, David began to cry, "Oh my son, Absalom, my son! Your rebellion has caused your death."

If only Absalom had been respectful, he would have had a good life. Instead, he rebelled against his father and God, and he ended up losing his life for it.

— Based on 2 Samuel 17:1–18:18

Discussion Questions

1. How did Absalom show his rebellion?
2. How can you show respect for your parents?

Authority Match-Up

puzzle

What You Need
- duplicated page
- crayons

What to Do
1. Duplicate a worksheet for each child.
2. Give each child a crayon to trace the lines from the authority figure to the item that describes that person.
3. Discuss each authority figure and explain why God wants us to show respect to and obey them.
4. Allow the children to color the pictures.

Respectful

68

David's Crown

What You Need
• jewels
• paper plates
• glue
• paintbrushes
• gold glitter

What to Do
1. Duplicate a set of jewels for each child.
2. Cut a slit down the center of each paper plate, starting about ½" from the outer rim on one edge and stopping about ½" from the outer rim on the opposite side of the plate. Cut three more slits to make eight pie-shaped sections.
3. Give each child a paintbrush.
4. Assist the children in painting glue on their plates and sprinkling gold glitter on them.
5. After the glue is dry, bend the crown triangles toward the rim.
6. Allow the children to color the jewels and glue one jewel on the end of each triangle point.

What To Say

King David was like our president. We should respect the president and pray for him so he will lead our country in a way that pleases God.

Respectful

69

Heart Plant

craft

What You Need
- duplicated page
- red craft foam
- foam cups
- craft sticks
- glue
- modeling clay

What to Do
1. Duplicate a cup wrap and face of Jesus for each child.
2. Use the heart pattern to cut hearts from red craft foam.
3. Instruct each child to glue a face of Jesus on a heart, and the heart on the end of a stick.
4. Allow each child to color a cup wrap and glue it around his or her cup.
5. Help each child put a piece of clay into the bottom of his or her cup, then push in the craft stick.

What to Say
Wherever Jesus is, respect grows. If you have Jesus in your heart, then you will remember to be respectful easily.

Respectful

back wrap

Where Jesus Is LOVE grows

Submit yourselves... to every authority. I Peter 2:13

Lunch Sack House

What You Need
- duplicated page
- paper lunch sacks
- crayons
- glue
- smiley stickers
- old newspapers
- stapler
- tape

What to Do
1. Duplicate and cut out the house pieces for each child.
2. Allow the children to color their house pieces.
3. Assist the children in gluing the pieces to the fronts of their sacks.
4. Instruct each child to put a smiley sticker over the door. Print each child's last name on his or her sticker.
5. Stuff the sacks with newspapers and staple the tops, covering the staples with tape to prevent injury. (If you plan to use the activity with "My Family Cutouts," on page 73, omit this step.)

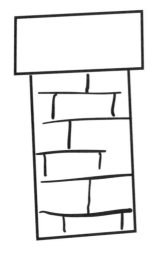

What To Say

God wants people to live in happy houses where they respect each other. Children should obey their parents, and be kind to each other.

Respectful

71

craft

What You Need
• duplicated page
• colored card stock
• chenille stems
• hole punch

What to Do
1. Duplicate the measuring spoons to colored card stock and cut out one set for each child. Cut the chenille stems in thirds.
2. Assist the children in punching a hole at the top of each spoon where indicated.
3. Give each child a chenille stem on which to slide the spoons. Assist in twisting the ends of the stems together.
4. Say the memory verse as you move the spoons from word to word. Although most of the children will not be able to read the memory verse words, they will enjoy pretending to read and moving the spoons.

Respectful

Measuring Spoon Verse

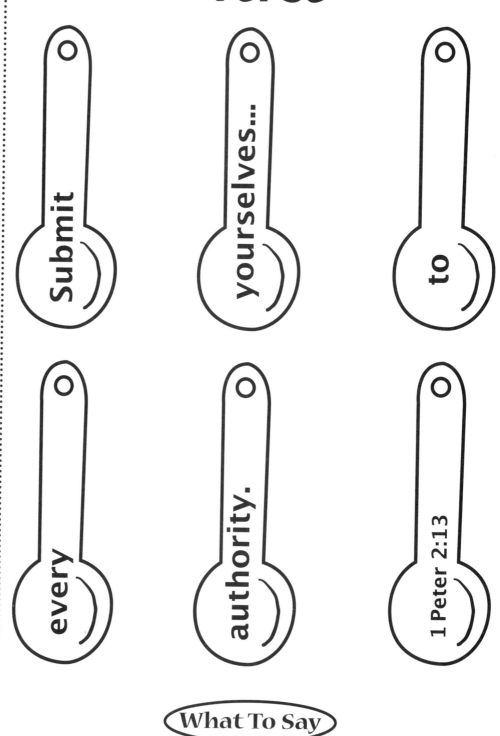

Submit

yourselves...

to

every

authority.

1 Peter 2:13

What To Say

One way to show respect is to be a helper. What can you do to help your father? How can you show respect to your mother?

My Family Cutouts

craft
. . . .

What You Need
• duplicated page
• crayons
• glue

What to Do
1. Duplicate the family cut-outs. If you are familiar with the children's families, copy pieces to match the members of their homes. If not, use a mother, father, boy and girl for each child.
2. Cut out the family cut-outs.
3. Allow the children to color their cut-outs, then sing the song together.
4. Sing the song to the tune of "When We All Work Together." Allow the children to hold up the family member about whom they are singing. Have each child store the pieces in his or her Lunch Sack House (page 71).

Continued on next page...

Respectful

Oh, I'll respect my mother, my mother, my mother.
Oh, I'll respect my mother, just like God said.
(Repeat with father)

Oh, I'll be kind to sister, to sister, to sister.
Oh I'll be kind to sister, just like God said.
(Repeat with brother)

Puzzled Heart Sticks

puzzle

What You Need
- duplicated page
- envelopes
- crayons

What to Do
1. Duplicate a puzzle for each child.
2. Before class, cut out the puzzles, placing each one in a separate envelope to keep the pieces together. Remove the center picture (of Jesus) from each one.
3. Give each child a puzzle to put together.

What to Say
The puzzles are complete except for the center picture. We need someone to help us show respect to our mommies, daddies, babysitters and grandparents.
Here are the pictures of Jesus for each of you. Now you can finish your puzzles. It's Jesus who helps us be respectful!

Respectful

craft

What You Need
• duplicated page
• craft sticks
• paint stirrer sticks (optional)
• glue
• crayons

What to Do
1. Duplicate and cut out a David and an Absalom picture for each child.
2. Allow the children to color the pictures.
3. Assist each child in gluing pictures around the top of craft sticks.
4. Instruct the children to hold up the Absalom picture when you are talking about Absalom, and King David when you talk about him.
5. Make a set of your own. Enlarge the pictures and use paint stirrer sticks instead of craft sticks. Tell the Bible story with the pictures.

Respectful

Story Picture Sticks

Chapter 8
God Wants Me to Be Kind, Not Discourteous

Memory Verse

Consider others better than yourselves.
Philippians 2:3

Story to Share
I'll Water Your Camels

Abraham thought it was time for his son Isaac to find a wife. He asked his most trusted servant to come see him.

"I want you to go back to the town where I was born," Abraham told his servant. "God will show you the girl He wants Isaac to marry."

So the servant left for Ur. He piled his camels with gifts to present to the chosen woman.

"How am I going to find the right wife for Isaac?" the servant wondered as he traveled along. "I know she should be a kind girl, and courteous."

The servant wasn't sure where to look for the right girl, so he prayed for God's help.

"When I stop at the well," he prayed, "I will ask a girl for water. If she is kind and offers water for my camels, too, I will know she is the one You have chosen for Isaac."

As the servant rode up to the well on his camel, he noticed one particularly beautiful girl. Her name was Rebekah.

Rebekah looked up and smiled at the servant. As he came down from his camel, he asked, "Will you draw me a drink of water?"

Rebekah quickly fetched a drink for the servant.

"Enjoy your drink, sir," she said to him. Then she drew more water for the camels.

The servant's heart began to pound. This courteous girl was the answer to his prayers. She was even kind to the animals!

The servant was happy when he returned with Rebekah for Isaac. He knew Abraham would be pleased. God had shown the servant the right wife for Isaac. Rebekah had a kind and loving heart — a heart for God.

— Based on Genesis 24:1-21

Discussion Questions

1. How was Rebekah kind and courteous to Abraham's servant?
2. How can you be kind and courteous to others?

Camel Jangles

craft

What You Need

- duplicated page
- construction paper
- crayons
- glue
- small jingle bells
- ribbon
- hole punch

What to Do

1. Duplicate and cut out a camel for each child. Punch holes where indicated.
2. Cut construction paper into 8" strips.
3. Allow the children to color their camels.
4. Instruct each child to glue a camel to the center of a paper strip.
5. Assist the children in threading ribbons through the holes on the camels and the jingle bells. Tie the ends in a knot, then in a bow.
6. Tape together the ends of the paper strips around the children's wrists.

Consider others better than yourselves. Phillippians 2:3

What To Say

When you wear your camel jangle, you will be reminded to be kind to others. God is happy when we are kind and not disrespectful.

Kind

78

Camel Kindness Time

It's camel kindness time.

It's camel kindness time.

It's camel kindness time.

It's camel kindness time.

It's camel kindness time.

It's camel kindness time.

What To Say

Every time your friends tilt their cups to take a drink and you see the camels, say, "It's camel kindness time!"

Camels eat dates, grass, oats and wheat – but if they're really hungry they forget to be kind and might eat bones or even their owner's tent! You can help your friends remember to be kind. When your friend or brother or sister forgets to be kind, you can say, "It's camel kindness time!"

snack

What You Need
- duplicated page
- clear, self-stick plastic
- whole dates
- peanut butter
- napkins
- plastic cups
- milk

What to Do
1. Duplicate and cut out a camel circle for each child.
2. Stuff whole dates with peanut butter.
3. Allow the children to color the drink circles. Print each child's name inside his or her camel.
4. Go around and cover the circles with clear plastic.
5. Allow each child to glue a drink circle to the bottom of his or her cup.
6. Fill cups with milk and serve stuffed dates on napkins.
7. Pray a prayer of thanks.
8. Wipe the cups so the children can take them home and re-use them.

Kind

song

What You Need
• duplicated page
• yellow paper
• yarn

What to Do
1. For each child, duplicate and cut out a bee picture on yellow paper.
2. Punch a hole at the top of each bee. Thread a length of yarn through each hole and tie the ends in a bow.
3. Give each child a bee. Print on the lines "(Hailey) is kind."
4. Sing the song to the tune of "Zacchaeus," instructing the children to hold up their bees when you come to the last two lines.

"Definition" Song

Philippians
2:3

Discourteous is a very big word,
A very big word indeed!
If you remember to be kind,
That big word you won't need.
Jesus said:
Don't hurt any of your friends!
Be kind as you can be.
Be kind as you can be.

I Care Kit

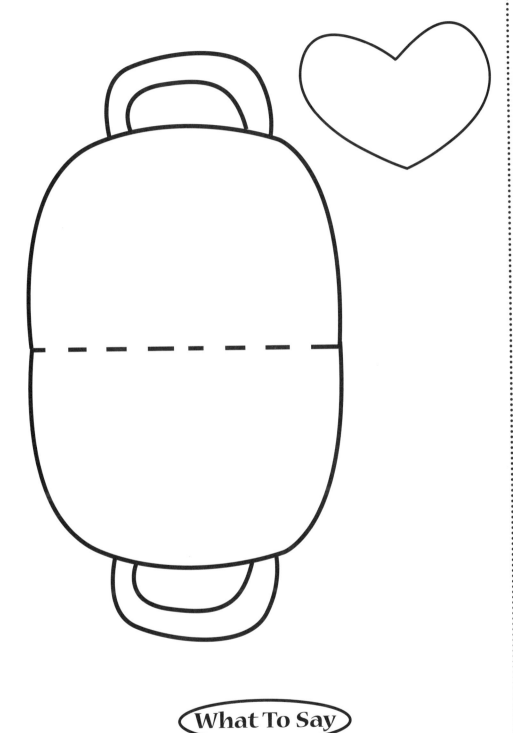

craft

What You Need
- duplicated page
- black craft foam
- red craft foam
- black electrical tape
- adhesive bandages
- glue
- permanent marker

What to Do
1. Trace and cut one doctor's kit from black foam and one heart from red foam for each child.
2. Fold and staple the sides of each kit together, covering the staples with black electrical tape to avoid injury.
3. Allow each child to glue a heart to the center of a kit.
4. On each child's heart write, "(Ethan's) Care Kit."
5. Give each child five bandages to place in his or her kit.
6. Let each child pretend to get hurt and another child show he or she cares by placing a bandage on the pretend injury.

What To Say

Sometimes when someone falls down we laugh. That makes the one who fell hurt even more. Let's make God happy by being kind and showing we care. Offer a bandage and a hug!

Kind

game

What You Need
- duplicated page
- glue

What to Do

1. Copy and cut out a bingo board, camel set and happy face markers for each child. Enlarge one set of camels to use as game pieces.

2. Instruct the children to glue their camel squares to their bingo boards in any sequence.

3. Demonstrate to the children how you will hold up a game piece and they will look to see where their matching camels are. Allow the children to cover their matching camels with happy face markers.

4. Each child who gets three happy face markers in a row should turn to the child beside him or her and say something kind.

Continued on
next page...

Kind

Kind Words Bingo

What To Say

When a child gets three markers in a row, say,
"Bingo! (Josh) just made God happy by being kind."

Peeking Verse Camels

Consider others better than yourselves.

Philippians 2:2

What You Need

- duplicated page
- tan construction paper
- safety scissors
- glue

What to Do

1. Duplicate the small camel to white paper, one for each child. Duplicate the large camel to tan construction paper, one for each child.
2. Cut out the tan camels.
3. Hide the tan camels around the room. Leave part of the camels's heads peeking out so the children can find them easily.
4. Choose a child to find a camel, then help the child say the memory verse. Then that child should choose a friend to find a camel. Continue until everyone has a camel.
5. Allow the children to cut out their verse camels and glue them to the backs of their tan camels.

Kind

What To Say

It took us a while to find all the camels, didn't it? It took Rebekah a while to water all the servant's camels, too. But she was being kind to her new friend. We should be kind and courteous to others, too.

Say Something Kind

puzzle

What You Need
- duplicated page
- pencils

What to Do
1. Duplicate a worksheet for each child.
2. For each set of pictures, read aloud the word bubble at the left, then tell how each child responds.
3. Instruct the children to circle the pictures of the children who are kind, and to draw "Xs" on those who are discourteous.

What to Say
When we are kind, we show we care about other people. God is happy when we are kind to others.

Kind

85

Twin Smile Dolls

craft

What You Need
- duplicated page
- crayons
- jumbo craft sticks
- brown and pink felt or flannel
- glue

What to Do
1. Duplicate and cut out a servant and Rebekah doll for each child.
2. Make a servant and Rebekah doll for yourself to aid you in telling the Bible story.
3. Allow the children to color the servant and Rebekah dolls and glue pieces of felt to their robes.
4. Assist each child in gluing the Rebekah doll to the back of the servant doll, sandwiching a craft stick in between.

Kind

What To Say

How do you think the servant felt when Rebekah gave him a drink of water? (happy – hold up happy servant) How do you think the servant felt when Rebekah watered his camels? (happy – hold up happy servant) How do you think Rebekah felt when she gave water to the servant and his camels? (happy – hold up happy Rebekah) Not only does kindness and courtesy make others happy, but we are happy when we help others, too.

Abel

Answer key for the Follow the Motions puzzle on page 9

In your anger do not sin.
Ephesians 4:26

craft

What You Need
- duplicated page
- wiggle eyes
- glue
- colored construction paper
- flesh colored paper
- flower stickers, Bible sticker

What to Do
1. Duplicate a set of body parts on flesh colored paper for each child and cut them out.
2. Cut construction paper sheets in half. Print each child's name on the top of a paper half.
3. At each class session, give each child a body part to glue to the construction paper (each wiggle eye counts as one).
4. Optional: give a flower sticker for each memory verse a child says. If a child says all eight verses, place a Bible sticker over the paper kid's heart.

More Ways to Be My Best

Attendance Booster

Classroom Border Kids

Happy	**Joyful**
Obedient	**Timely**
Honest	**Patient**
Respectful	**Kind**

What You Need

- duplicated page and page 90
- skin-tone paper
- bright card stock
- yarn scraps
- fabric scraps
- lace scraps
- buttons
- wiggle eyes
- glue
- markers

What to Do

1. Duplicate the border kids to various shades of skin-tone paper, and the virtue words to card stock.
2. Allow the children to "dress" the border kids using fabric, wiggle eyes and other items.
3. Cut out the virtue words.
4. Attach the dolls to the middle of your classroom walls (or around a bulletin board): a girl doll, then a virtue, a boy doll, then a virtue.
5. Add a doll each class for each child present. See how many classes it takes to get around the room.

More Ways to Be My Best

craft

What You Need
• duplicated page
• heavy card stock
• sandpaper
• crayons
• cinnamon sticks

What to Do
1. Duplicate the kid patterns to heavy card stock and cut out a boy or girl for each child.
2. Trace the kids face down on sandpaper and cut out one sandpaper kid for each child.
3. Allow the children to color their kids.
4. Instruct the children to glue their sandpaper kids to the backs of their kids.
5. Give each child a cinnamon stick.
6. Show how to rub the cinnamon over the sandpaper.

What to Say
When others notice us being kind, respectful and obedient, they are reminded of a pleasant smell. Your good behavior reminds your friends of Jesus.

More Ways to Be My Best

Cinnamon Kid

I'm a Jesus Kid Badge

Teacher Help

teacher help

What You Need
- duplicated page
- clear, self-stick plastic
- ribbon
- hole punch
- crayons

What to Do
1. Duplicate and cut out a badge for each child.
2. Print each child's name on a badge.
3. Allow the children to color their badges.
4. Assist the children in covering the fronts and backs of their badges with clear, self-stick plastic.
5. Punch a hole at the top of each badge. Thread a necklace-length ribbon through each hole and tie the ends together.
6. Give each child his or her badge to wear each Sunday. Look at the leftover badges to know who was not in class that week.

More Ways to Be My Best

I'm being my best for

I'm being my best for

Kid Contact Tool

teacher help

What You Need
- duplicated page
- bright paper
- stamps
- envelopes

What to Do
1. Duplicate the cards to bright paper.
2. Write any absentee children's names and addresses on the envelopes.
3. Allow the children to sign the cards (if they can print) or draw a tiny heart or other object (and you can print their names beside them).
4. Put stamps on the envelopes and drop them in the mail. This is a good tool for keeping your children coming to class.

More Ways to Be My Best

Come Learn
How To Be
Your Best
For God!

Kid Helpers

teacher help

. . . .

What You Need
- duplicated page
- crayons
- craft sticks
- cup
- glue

What to Do
1. Duplicate and cut out a kid shape for each child.
2. Print each child's name on a kid.
3. Allow the children to color their kids.
4. Assist each child in gluing a craft stick to the back of his or her kid.
5. Place each kid-shape in the cup. When you need help holding a song, passing out napkins or picking up the trash, choose a kid from the cup. When the cup is empty, you will know everyone has had an opportunity to be a helper.

More Ways to Be My Best

craft

What You Need
- duplicated page
- black construction paper
- white paper
- crayons
- gold cross stickers
- gold ink pen
- stapler
- tape

What to Do
1. Trace the large Bible to black construction paper. Cut out and fold in half a Bible for each child. Write each child's name at the bottom of a Bible cover in gold ink.
2. Trace the inside line on the Bible and cut it out for a pattern. Trace the pattern to white paper and cut out two for each child. Fold the pages together and staple them to the insides of the Bible covers. Cover the staples with tape to prevent injury.
3. Duplicate and cut out the letters.

Continued at right...

More Ways to Be My Best

Memory Verse Book

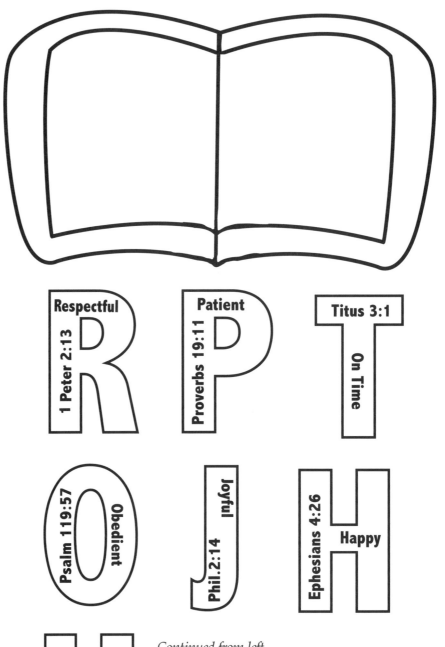

Respectful
1 Peter 2:13
R

Patient
Proverbs 19:11
P

Titus 3:1
On Time
T

Psalm 119:57
Obedient
O

Phil.2:14
Joyful
J

Ephesians 4:26
Happy
H

Colossians 3:9
Honest
H

Continued from left...

4. Give each child a Bible and a cross to stick on the front of it.
5. Each week, allow each child to color the letter that corresponds to the verse of the day, and glue the letter to a page.
6. At the end of the *Being My Best for God* lessons, give each child his or her Bible to take home.

What to Say
These are important verses for you to remember. Ask your mommy or daddy to read these verses to you.

Virtues at Home

BEING MY BEST FOR GOD

happy, joyful, obedient, timely, honest, patient, respectful, and kind

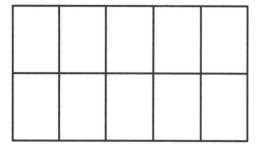

Dear Parent,

This is your child's Being My Best for God Poster. When you catch your child being patient or exhibiting any of the other virtues, draw a smiley face in one of the boxes. When your child has 10 smiley faces, give him or her a special treat.

If you do something over and over it will become a habit. Practice being happy, joyful, obedient, timely, honest, patient, respectful, and kind – then you will know you are being your best for God!

What You Need

• duplicated page
• construction paper
• self-stick magnets
• glue
• crayons
• yarn

What to Do

1. Duplicate a poster and parent letter for each child.
2. Give each child a sheet of construction paper, a poster and a letter.
3. Allow each child to glue a poster on the front of the construction paper and a letter on the back.
4. Instruct each child to attach magnets to the four corners of the letter side.
5. Send a poster home with each child. If desired, punch a hole near the top of each poster and tie an 8" length of yarn through the hole, then tie a crayon to the opposite end.

More Ways to Be My Best

Wiggle Buster

What You Need
• duplicated page

What to Do
1. Sing the song to the tune of "Fishers of Men."
2. This would be a good song to sing before the Bible story of any chapter – just change the word "kind" to the chapter's topic: happy, joyful, obedient, timely, honest, patient or respectful.

I (touch head)
will learn (touch shoulders)
'bout kids (hands on hips)
just like me.
    (shake hands in front of you)
Kids just like me,
    (shake hands in front of you)
kids just like me.
    (shake hands in front of you)
I (touch head)
will learn (touch shoulders)

'bout kids (hands on hips)
just like me,
    (shake hands in front of you.)
From (touch knees)
God's Holy Word. (touch toes)

I will learn to be so (kind),
Be so (kind), be so (kind).
I will learn to be so (kind),
From God's Holy Word.

More Ways to Be My Best

96